Ice Hockey Rulebook

Contents

Origins

'You miss 100 percent of the shots you never take.'
Wayne Gretzky

No one can say for sure when the best sport ever created – hockey – came into being, but it is known that its roots lie in northern Europe over five hundred years ago.

At the time field hockey was a popular summer sport and when ponds and lakes froze over during winter months some players developed an alternative version of it on ice. One such adaptation is a game called *kolven*, which was first played in the Netherlands in the seventeenth century and later became popular in England.

Better known today is the rise of hockey's popularity in North America.

In the 1870s British troops in Nova Scotia and students at Montreal's McGill University started playing organised hockey matches on frozen ponds, shortly followed by the creation of North America's first hockey league in Kingston, Ontario in 1885.

Soon, clubs from the key Canadian cities of Toronto, Montreal and Ottawa were frequently playing matches against one another, and the Governor General of Canada, Lord Frederick Stanley, was so impressed that he had a silver bowl made in 1892 to be presented annually to the best amateur hockey team in the country.

Today this bowl is known as the Stanley Cup, and is widely hailed as the Holy Grail of all hockey trophies – being awarded to whichever team wins the annual National Hockey League playoffs.

At the turn of the twentieth century, hockey went from being a purely amateur sport to a professional one when the short-lived International Professional Hockey League and National Hockey Association were created in 1904 and 1907 respectively.

It was during the First World War, however, that the predominant hockey league in the world today was created.

Upon its formation, the National Hockey League (or NHL) consisted of five franchises – the Montreal Canadiens, the Montreal Wanderers, the Ottawa Senators, the Quebec Bulldogs, and the Toronto Arenas – and held its first match on 19th December 1917. Since then it has grown to a 31-team-strong league (soon to be 32 with the admission of a Seattle franchise), and is one of North America's four principal sports organisations – along with the National Football League, the National Basketball Association, and Major League Baseball. And if it is to be judged on its pace, physicality, passion, and pageantry it is also the best. Because, to use the words of the legendary Jack Edwards, hockey players possess one thing soccer players severely lack: 'hearts of lions'.

Rules

The ultimate aim in hockey – like many other team sports – is to score more goals than the opposing team by shooting or redirecting the puck into the net.

Each play begins with a face-off and is halted when a referee or linesman blows the whistle (to call a goal, icing, frozen puck, offside, or penalty).

Games consist of three 20 minute periods, and each team has five skaters (one centre, two wingers, and two defencemen) and one goalie on the ice at any one time. In the event of a tie, NHL matches are decided by a five-minute three-versus-three overtime period where the first goal scored wins the game. If the overtime period is scoreless, the game proceeds to a shootout in which each team gets three shots (and after that one shot each).

In the NHL teams play eighteen skaters (four forward units of three players, and three defensive units of two players) and two goaltenders (one starter and one reserve) in each match. Teams in many other leagues, however, are usually limited to three forward units.

*

While hockey has many rules to ensure player safety and to manage the pace and flow of matches, the four essential rules for playing the game are easy to learn and follow:

- **Face-offs:** Face-offs are used to begin every game, period and play. It involves a referee (at the start of a game) or linesman (during the game) dropping the puck between the sticks of two opposing players. The opposing players then fight for possession of the puck. There are nine face-off dots on the rink where face-offs may take place depending on where and under what circumstances play was halted (one at centre ice; two near each blue line, just inside the neutral zone; and two in the offensive and defensive zones). Players can be tossed from a face-off and replaced with a teammate if a player is not positioned properly or does not have the blade of their stick on the ice.

- **Icing:** This refers to when an attacking player shoots/passes the puck into the offensive zone before passing the halfway (red) line. If one of the attacking player's teammates does not touch the puck before it passes the goal line, play is halted and a face-off takes place in the offending party's defensive zone. This rule helps to keep the game moving and prevent teams from trying to run the clock down (although teams playing shorthanded are allowed to dump the puck into the offensive zone as many times as they like without facing an icing call).
- **Offside:** If an attacking player crosses into the offensive zone before the puck then play is stopped and a face-off is called at one of the four blue line face-off dots. *Both* skates must be all the way over the blue line before the puck for the play to be ruled offside. This prevents players from goal hanging and obtaining easy breakaways. In some leagues the flow of the game is enhanced by allowing 'delayed' offsides. These take place if an attacking player dumps the puck into their offensive zone while one or more of their teammates is already in the offensive zone. If all the attacking players leave the offensive zone without touching the puck then the delayed offside is waived and play continues without stoppage.
- **Frozen puck:** This involves covering the puck to force a stoppage in play. This is most commonly performed by goaltenders to prevent attacking players from getting a rebound.

Other important things to know include:

- **Scoring:** In order to record a goal, a player must shoot or redirect the puck in between the goalposts and completely over the red goal line. However, goals can be disallowed if there was interference with the netminder, if an attacking player deliberately bats or kicks the puck into the goal with part of their body, or if they redirect it with their stick above the height of the crossbar.
When a goal is scored, the referee officially awards it by blowing their whistle and pointing towards the net.

- **Periods:** As has already been mentioned, NHL games are divided into three 20-minute periods, and teams change sides at the start of each period. If the contest is tied at the end of regulation time during the regular season, teams play an additional period of sudden-death overtime that lasts no more than five minutes, with each side having only three skaters and a goaltender. The club that scores first wins. If no one scores, the game is decided by a shootout – the best of three shots, and then one vs. one shots if it is still tied after the first three. During the playoffs, however, the overtime continues until a deciding goal is scored, with the teams breaking every 20 minutes as they do during regular play.

- **Substitutions:** Skaters on the bench can enter the game while play is in progress as long as the player they are changing with is within five feet of the bench (if they do not meet this criteria, the team will be assessed a two minute minor penalty for too many men on the ice). Players can also be swapped during stoppages in play. In this instance the visiting team is allowed a reasonable amount of time (5-10 seconds) to make changes, before the home team does the same (giving the latter an advantage). Goaltenders can be switched at any time, although they are only granted a warm-up in the rare occasion that they are the third goaltender (with the starting and back-up goaltenders having both been knocked out of the game).

Rink

Traditionally, hockey was played on frozen ponds, lakes and rivers, with snow being piled up to serve as boundaries.

Today pond hockey still exists, but organised hockey is played in indoor rinks. The area of play is surrounded by boards that must measure between 40 and 48 inches tall. To allow play to be viewed, the rink is also surrounded by synthetic glass (except for the area in front of the two teams' benches to allow skaters to jump in and out of play).

Dimensions

The standard NHL rink measures 200 feet long by 85 feet wide.

Rinks used for international competition are slightly larger, measuring 200 feet long by 100 feet wide. A larger playing surface promotes open play and gives the game greater flow but also takes away much of the physical play that North American fans enjoy to watch.

Zones

Neutral zone: The area of the ice in between the blue lines where teams transition from offence to defence.

Offensive zone: The portion of the ice where the opposing team's goal is.

Defensive zone: The portion of the ice where a team is trying to prevent goals being scored.

Lines

Goal line: The goal line is red in colour and is at the far end of both the offensive and defensive zones. This line passes in front of the goal (the puck must cross this line for it to be counted as a goal) and is used for icing calls (icing cannot be called on a dump-in from behind the halfway line until the puck passes this line).

Blue line: The blue lines separate the offensive and defensive zones from the neutral zone. The puck must cross this line into the offensive zone before attacking players can enter, otherwise offside will be called.

Red line: The red line runs along the middle of the rink and divides the ice in half. Hockey games begin with face-offs from the centre dot in the middle of this line (with face-offs always being held here at the start of new periods and after goals are scored).

Face-off dots

There are nine dots on the ice where face-offs can take place: one at centre ice, four in the neutral zone along the blue lines, two in the offensive zone, and two in the defensive zone. The dots at centre ice and in the offensive and defensive zones are surrounded by circles. Only the players taking the face-off (usually centres) are allowed inside the circle prior to the puck being dropped.

Goal

A standard hockey goal measures six feet wide by four feet tall.

Goalie Trapezoid

A section behind the goal, marked off by red lines. The goalie cannot play the puck outside of this area behind the goal line. If they defy this rule their team will be assessed a two minute minor penalty for delay of game.

Goal crease

This is marked by a blue semi-circle and is an area where attacking players are not able to interfere with the goaltender. Furthermore, attacking players are only allowed in this area if the puck is loose in the blue paint. If a player scores a goal while interfering with a goaltender in the goal crease the goal will be disallowed.

Referee crease

This is a marked-off section to allow the on-ice officials to speak with the scorer or timekeeper without interruption. If the referee is talking to an off-ice official, players are not permitted to enter this crease.

Bench

The bench is where players sit who are not in play. There are separate benches for the home and road teams and players can enter and exit play by using a door at either end of the bench or by jumping over the boards.

Penalty box

The penalty box is an enclosed booth, usually next to the scorer and timekeeper's box. Players who have received a penalty must sit here for its duration.

Positions

In hockey matches teams can have five skaters and a goaltender on the ice at any one time.

The position an individual plays is typically determined by their size and skillset – with faster players normally serving as forwards and bigger, more physically imposing individuals playing defence.

Centre

The centre is essentially a team's quarterback. They are responsible for taking face-offs and covering the middle of the ice at both ends of the rink. They typically skate greater distances than other positions as they are expected to direct play in both the offensive and defensive zones.

Although centres come in different shapes and sizes and have a variety of playing styles, they usually have the following characteristics in common:

- Strong on face-offs
- Good passing/shooting skills
- Able to lead at both ends of the ice

The first-line centre is typically one of the team's highest scorers (because they can pass and shoot well), and most second-line centres have strong offensive capabilities too. Third and fourth-line centres, on the other hand, are generally expected to be good at taking face-offs and strong checkers in order to prevent the opposing team's top two lines from getting on the scoresheet.

Winger

Right and left wingers tend to play along the boards on their respective sides of the ice, and are primarily relied upon to score goals.

Traditionally right wingers were right-handed shots and left wingers were left-handed shots, although this is not always the case in the modern game. Having left-handed shots playing on the right side and vice versa gives the player a better chance of one-timing shots without breaking stride, which can be a very effective way of scoring a goal.

Wingers have a variety of playing styles, including: playmaker (specialises in passing and making plays), power forward (excels in physical aspects of the game as well as contributing offensively), sniper (fast skaters with accurate shots, allowing them to score lots of goals), two-way forward (proficient in both offensive and defensive aspects of the game), and grinder (a physical presence, used to intimidate opposing players, protect teammates, and generate energy).

While the most offensively talented wingers typically play on the top two lines, more defensive-minded wingers are placed on the third line and enforcers fill the fourth line spots (using their limited ice time to hit hard, create turnovers, and motivate their team).

Defence

The main jobs of defencemen are to protect the goaltender, and to prevent opposing players from taking shots on goal by either blocking shots or cutting them off from preferable shooting angles. It is therefore important that defenders are physically dominating.

When playing in the offensive zone, they typically remain just inside the blue line in case a counterattack is launched by the opposing team.

However, defenders do have an offensive role too. After clearing the puck out of their defensive zone it is normally a defender who makes the first pass to start an offensive rush up the ice. This first play can be decisive in determining whether the rush is successful or not, and in rare occasions – such as Bobby Orr – defenders can be leading scorers on their team.

Goaltender

Unsurprisingly, the goaltender's job is to prevent the puck from going in the net, and they remain in their crease for the entire game.

As well as being excellent skaters and stickhandlers, agility and athleticism are also key due to the fact that they have to scramble around with so much equipment on. Good instincts and concentration are also a must for any successful goalie, given that one minor lapse in concentration can be the difference between winning or losing a game.

There is little doubt that goaltenders play the most specialised position in hockey, and this is reflected by the uniqueness of the equipment they wear in order to provide better protection from the puck.

Officials

In the NHL each game is officiated by two referees and two linesmen.

Referees are considered the main on-ice official and can be identified by the orange armbands they wear. They are responsible for supervising the entire match, including dropping the puck at the start of each game, calling penalties and settling disputes.

The principal responsibility of linesmen, on the other hand, is to make offside and icing calls, and to conduct all face-offs after the opening. They are also expected to act as an extra pair of eyes and ears for the referees – calling penalties in some circumstances and helping to break up fights.

Other notable mentions include official scorers and goal judges.

While official scorers record the game's stats (including shots, saves, goals, assists and penalties), goal judges are responsible for reporting when the puck crosses the goal line. Traditionally, there is one goal judge based at each end of the ice, although modern technology has changed the role. Today many goal judges are not based at ice-level and monitor the goal area via video feed.

Penalties

There are a wide range of penalties that can be called in hockey. Each is classified as a type of penalty, as well as being designated a level of severity.

Penalties fall under five broad categories:

Minor: This lasts for two minutes, and is by far the most common form of penalty. The offending player must sit in the penalty box until the penalty time expires or the opposing team scores.

Double minor: This consists of two back-to-back two-minute minor penalties. Double minors are normally called if a player commits two minor offences or if a single offence is too serious to be a minor.

Major: This lasts for five minutes, and the offending player must remain in the penalty box for the full length of the penalty even if the opposing team scores. These are reserved for more serious violations, such as fighting.

Misconduct: These are served for ten minutes by the offending player, although in most leagues their team will only have to play five of these minutes shorthanded. There are three broad types of misconduct penalty that can be given:

- Basic misconduct: These can be given for acts such as shouting at an official. The player is forced to sit in the penalty box for ten minutes, but there is no manpower change.
- Game misconduct: When a player is tossed from the game, usually for delivering a dangerous check to a vulnerable player.
- Gross misconduct: When a player is tossed from the game and can potentially face more serious league action (including fines and suspensions from future games).

Penalty shot: These can be called if a player is on a breakaway and is tripped or restrained from behind by illegal contact. The offended player is given a one-on-one confrontation with the goaltender. To call a penalty shot the official crosses their arms above their head with their fists clenched.

Delayed penalties occur when a team commits an offence worthy of a penalty but does not gain possession of the puck. Play will only be stopped and the penalty called when a player from the offending team touches the puck. If the delayed penalty is for a *minor* offence and the fouled team scores before play is halted, the penalty is waved off.

A delayed penalty is marked by an official extending their non-whistle-holding hand in the air.

*

There are many types of penalties that can be called in hockey games, with the punishment being determined by the severity of the act (e.g. intent to cause injury is likely to lead to a misconduct).

Some of the most notable penalties include:

Boarding: When a player pushes, trips or checks an opponent violently into the boards. Officials call this by crossing their forearms.

Charging: When a player takes extra strides to gain momentum before checking an opponent. Officials call this by rotating clenched fists around one another in front of the chest.

Checking from behind: When a player hits an opponent who is not aware of the impending contact, therefore denying them the opportunity of defending themselves. Officials call this with the palms of the hands open and facing away from the body, fully extended from the chest at shoulder level.

Cross-checking: Using the shaft of a stick to check a player. Officials call this with both fists clenched and extending from the chest.

Delay of game: This can be called if a player purposefully tosses the puck over the glass and out of play, or if a goaltender handles the puck outside the goalie trapezoid. Officials call this using the non-whistle-holding hand (palm open), which is placed across the chest and then fully extended directly in front of the body.

Elbowing: Checking an opponent with an extended elbow. Officials call this by tapping either elbow with the other hand.

Fighting: When players drop their gloves (to inflict maximum pain with their bare knuckles) and fight each other. Officials call this with a double punching motion. The fist is clenched and fully extended in front of the body.

High-sticking: Any contact made by a stick on an opponent above the shoulders. Officials call this by holding both fists clenched, one immediately above the other at the height of the shoulders.

Hooking: Using the blade of the stick to restrain an opponent. Officials call this with a tugging motion with both arms, as if pulling something from in front of the stomach.

Holding: Using the arms to restrain an opponent. Officials call this by clasping either wrist with the other hand in front of the chest.

Interference: When a player impedes the progress of an opponent who does not have the puck. Officials call this by crossing their arms with closed fists stationary in front of the chest.

Roughing: Unnecessary physical contact, such as shoving or punching an opponent, that is not serious enough to be deemed worthy of a major penalty. Officials call this with a clenched fist and an arm extended out of the side of the body.

Slashing: Using the stick to chop at an opponent's body, stick or hands in order to impede their progress or to cause injury. Officials call this using a chopping motion with the edge of one hand across the opposite forearm.

Spearing: When a player thrusts their stick into an opposing player. Officials call this using a jabbing motion with both hands thrust out directly in front of the body.

Too many men on the ice: When a team has more than the legal number of players (six, including the goalie, if not playing short-handed) on the ice at one time. Officials call this by holding up six fingers.

Tripping: When a player uses their stick, foot, leg or arm to trip an opponent. Officials call this by striking the right leg with the right hand below the knee.

Unsportsmanlike conduct: When a player is penalised for disorderly conduct, such as subjecting an official or opposing player to verbal abuse. Officials call this by using both hands to form a 'T' in front of the chest.

*

While a penalty is being served, the opposing team receives a man advantage opportunity called a power-play.

Officials can send as many players as they like to the penalty box. However, teams always have a minimum of three players on the ice at any one time.

If a goaltender commits a penalty, a skater will be selected to serve the penalty for them.

Equipment

While in the old days players and goalies alike wore little to no padding, in the modern game players wear a range of protective equipment to prevent injury from pucks, sticks and collisions.

As you will see below, a goaltender's gear is drastically different to that worn by skaters.

Skaters are equipped with the following:

- Skates
- Stick
- Gloves
- Helmet
- Shoulder pads
- Box
- Pants
- Shin guards
- Elbow pads

Goalies wear:

- Goalie skates
- Goalie stick
- Mask
- Leg pads
- Catching glove
- Blocker
- Box
- Pants
- Chest and arm protection

Puck

According to Rule 25 of the NHL rulebook a puck should meet the following criteria:

'The puck shall be made of vulcanised rubber, or other approved material, one inch thick and three inches in diameter and shall weigh between five and one-half ounces and six ounces.'

Skates

Skates are undoubtedly the most important piece of equipment for all hockey players.

The boots were traditionally made out of leather, but in recent years manufacturers have started to use a combination of materials. The interiors are often made of a synthetic leather called Clarino that is easier to break in and more water-resistant, while the exteriors are composed of materials such as graphite which help to keep the boot light, stiff and durable.

Goalie skates are made of the same materials to those worn by skaters, but have a different shape and design – including wider blades and a plastic shell on the outside to provide better protection from pucks.

Skate blades can be adjusted by sharpening, and different players will have the edges sharpened to a radius that suits their assets and position of play. A smaller radius enables skaters to dig deeper into the ice, allowing tighter turns and faster acceleration. However, due to the friction digging deeper into the ice creates, it also makes the skater slower. A larger radius, therefore, maximises speed and minimises fatigue, but comes at the price of more limited manoeuvrability.

Most adults purchase skates that are a size to a size and a half smaller than their usual shoe size, while children typically drop half a size. This helps to ensure they fit snugly around your feet. In order to make sure it's the right fit at the time of purchase, push your toe to the front of the skate and put a finger down behind the heel. If you can fit more than one finger in there, the skate is too big.

Sticks

While hockey sticks are traditionally made out of wood the majority of sticks on sale today feature aluminium, graphite, Kevlar, or titanium shafts into which wooden blades are inserted. These blades are curved to give shots and passes more lift and power.

Sticks come in a range of lengths and flexes. More offensive-minded players tend to favour having shorter sticks so they can keep the puck close to their body, whereas defensive players tend to have longer sticks to give them maximum reach when poke-checking players. With regards to flex, meanwhile, forwards tend to use more flexible sticks (as they tend to use snap and wrist shots close to the net), while defenders normally favour stiffer sticks (to enhance the power of their shots when taking long-range slap-shots from the blue line).

Protection

The remainder of a hockey player's equipment is designed primarily to protect them from pucks, sticks and body-checks, while allowing as much speed and manoeuvrability as possible.

It is compulsory for all players to wear helmets, and for junior players to wear face masks/cages. Older players may play with a clear facial visor to allow them some protection while maintaining visibility.

Shoulder pads vary in size to meet the needs of individual players, with defencemen typically preferring heavier pads due to their role involving more checking than players in other positions.

Other padding worn by players includes a box/cup, padded pants, shin guards, elbow pads, and gloves. All these should fit snugly, and not be too loose.

<u>Goalie gear</u>

Goalies wear masks as well as helmets to offer greater protection from the puck. They also have additional neck protection, and thicker padding on their chests, arms and wrists. They wear large pillow-like pads on both legs, and their gloves are noticeably different to those worn by skaters: having a *blocker* on their stickhandling hand, and a *catcher* (which looks a little like an oversized baseball glove) on the other.

Jargon

Assist: Attributed to up to two players who contribute to the scoring of a goal by passing or setting up a deflection.

Backcheck: When players rush back to their defensive zone in response to attack by the opposing team.

Backhand: A pass or shot that is taken from the backside of the blade of the stick.

Bar down: When the puck hits the crossbar and goes in the net.

Biscuit: Puck

Blocker: A rectangular pad worn by goaltenders on their stick-holding hand.

Blue line: The lines separating the attacking/defending zones from the neutral zone.

Body check: When a player uses their body to knock an opponent off the puck.

Breakaway: When a player has possession of the puck and there are no defenders other than the goalie between them and the opposing goal.

Butterfly: A style of goaltending in which the goaltender drops to their knees and covers the lower half of the net with their leg pads.

Cage: A metal grid that attaches to the front of a helmet to protect the face. It is also occasionally used to refer to the goal.

Catching glove: A webbed glove that goaltenders wear on their non-stick-holding hand.

Change on the fly: Substitute a player from the bench during live play.

Crashing the net: When a player skates at full speed towards the front of the net (usually with intention of finding a rebound or loose puck).

Cycling: An offensive strategy used to maintain control of the puck by keeping it close the boards. Offensive players make short passes to each other along the boards until they see an opening to pass to a teammate who is moving into the slot for a shot on goal.

Dangle: When a player performs a series of dekes to get around an opposing player(s).

Defensive zone: The portion of the ice where a team's goal is situated. This extends from the blue line to the end boards.

Deke: When a player handles the puck in a way that fools a defending player into moving in the wrong direction.

Delayed penalty: A penalty that has not yet resulted in a stoppage of play because the team that will have the man advantage is still in possession of the puck. Play continues until the team being penalized gains control of the puck. The referee will raise their arm to indicate there is a delayed penalty.

Dump and chase: An offensive strategy used to get the puck into the offensive zone and into the corners where players can race to get it.

Even strength: When both teams have an equal number of players on the ice.

Extra attacker: A player who has been substituted for the team's goaltender on the ice.

Face-off: The method used to start play at the beginning of a period or after a stoppage of play. This involves one player from each team (usually centres) attempting to gain control of the puck after it is dropped by an official between their sticks onto a face-off spot on the ice.

Face-off spot: One of nine painted circles/spots on the ice where a face-off may take place.

Five-hole: The gap between a goaltender's legs.

Forecheck: Checking in the offensive zone in order to gain control of the puck and create a scoring opportunity.

Full strength: When both teams have five skaters and one goaltender on the ice.

Gordie Howe hat trick: When a player records a goal, assist, and fight in a single game.

Goal crease: An area of the ice that extends from the goal line in front of the net, often shaped like a semicircle and painted blue.

Goal line: The line that extents from the post to the boards. In order to score a goal the puck must cross this line in front of the net.

Golden goal: An overtime game-winning goal.

Hand pass: Passing the puck using one's hand. This is permitted inside a team's defensive zone, but is illegal in the neutral and offensive zones.

Hat-trick: When a player scores three goals in one game. Fans often throw hats onto the ice when this happens.

Head fake: A quick tilt of the head in one direction, followed by a quick move in the opposite direction to deceive an opponent.

Healthy scratch: An uninjured player on a team's roster who is not selected to play in a given game.

Hip check: Where a player uses their hip to knock an opponent against the boards or to the ice.

Light the lamp: Score a goal.

Line brawl: A series of fights involving most (or all) of the players on the ice.

Line change: When a team switches their forwards and/or defencemen, in order to keep their players fresh or to match certain players against certain opposing players. These can take place during play or between whistles.

Man advantage: When a team is penalised and one of its players is sent to the penalty box, giving the opposing team a numerical advantage for the duration of the penalty.

Natural hat-trick: When a player scores three consecutive goals or three goals in a single period.

Netminder: Goalie

Neutral zone: This is situated in between the two blue lines (and the offensive and defensive zones).

Odd-man rush: When a team enters the offensive zone and outnumbers the defending players in the zone.

One-timer: Shooting the puck directly off a pass.

Offensive zone: The portion of the ice where the opposition's goal is situated. This extends from the blue line to the end boards.

Paddle: The wide portion above the blade of a goaltender's stick.

Penalty box: The area where players sit to serve penalties.

Penalty kill: When a team has less players than their opponent due to a penalty against them.

Plus-minus: A statistic where a player receives +1 when they are on the ice when a goal is scored by their team (except when they are on the power play) and gets a -1 when they are on the ice when their team concedes a goal (except when they are shorthanded).

Poke check: Using the stick to poke the puck off an opponent's stick.

Power play: When a team has more players on the ice than their opponent due to a penalty being called.

Red Line: The line marking the middle of the ice surface.

Saucer pass: A technique in which the puck is passed to another player in such a way that it flies in the air like a flying saucer. This makes the pass very difficult to intercept by opposing players but it will still land flat on the ice, allowing the receiving player to handle it with ease.

Screened shot: A shot that the goaltender cannot see due to other players obscuring it.

Shorthanded: When a team has less players on the ice than their opponent due to a penalty.

Shortie: A goal scored by a team while shorthanded.

Shortside: The side of the goal closest to the shooter.

Shutout: When a goaltender does not concede any goals in a game.

Sin bin: Penalty box

Slap shot: A hard shot taken by winding up and slapping the puck towards the net.

Slew foot: Sweeping or kicking out a player's skate or tripping them from behind, causing them to fall backwards.

Slot: An area of the rink, situated in front of the goaltender and between the face-off circles on each side.

Snap shot: A very accurate, quick shot accomplished with a quick snap of the wrists.

Special teams: A collective term for the players that play on the power play and shorthanded units.

Spin-o-rama: Where a player completes one or several tight circles with the puck on their stick, eluding pursuing opponents.

Split the D: When an offensive player confuses or outmanoeuvres two defencemen in order to get between them.

Stack the pads: A save where the goaltender drops to one side and makes a save with their leg pads stacked on top of each other.

Stick check: Using the stick to interfere with an opposing player's stick and strip them of the puck.

Toe drag: When a player uses the toe of the stick to pull the puck closer to their body and out of reach of an opponent.

Trapper: Catching glove

Wheelhouse: The area immediately at a player's feet and in line with the player's shoulders (the optimum location for a player to get the most power from a slap-shot).

Wraparound: A scoring chance when a player has the puck behind the net, skates quickly around the side and tries to sneak the puck past the goaltender into the net.

Wrist shot: A quick shot that's fired off by pressure on the stick and a flick of the wrist.

Zamboni: Used to resurface the ice.

Printed in Great Britain
by Amazon